ONLINE LEGAL RESEARCH

To Accompany

LEGAL RESEARCH: A PRACTICAL GUIDE AND SELF-INSTRUCTIONAL WORKBOOK
(5th Ed. 2008)

Supplement by

AMY FLANARY-SMITH

RUTH ANN McKINNEY

SCOTT CHILDS

The University of North Carolina School of Law
Chapel Hill, North Carolina

THOMSON-WEST

ST. PAUL, MINN., 2008

Cover Image: Bret M. Gerbe
Cover Design: Carol Dungan Logie, Avatar Creative
Book Design and Layout: Claudia Fulshaw Design

The West Group symbol is a trademark
registered in the U.S. Patent and Trademark Office.

COPYRIGHT © 1996 WEST PUBLISHING CO.
© West, a Thomson business, 2000, 2001, 2003
© 2008 Thomson/West
      610 Opperman Drive
      St. Paul, MN 55123
      1–800–313–9378
Printed in the United States of America

ISBN: 978–0–314–18501–3

 TEXT IS PRINTED ON 10% POST CONSUMER RECYCLED PAPER

Acknowledgments

The authors warmly acknowledge the work of Philip K. Woods, author of the original Computer Assisted Legal Research Problem Set published in 2000. We are most appreciative for his generosity in allowing us to build on the strong foundation he established.

We are indebted to the teaching faculty and staff of the Kathrine R. Everett Law Library of the University of North Carolina School of Law as well as the teaching faculty and staff of the Research, Reasoning, Writing, and Advocacy Program for their collegial assistance on this and many other projects.

Finally, we thank our spouses for their patience with, encouragement of, and enthusiasm for the work that we do.

Table of Contents

I. Chapter 4*: The Process of Legal Research Revisited

II. Assigning Memo 6

* Chapters 1-3, as well as exercises in hard copy materials, can be found in the main workbook that this Supplement accompanies: Ruth Ann McKinney & Scott Childs, Legal Research: A Practical Guide and Self-Instructional Workbook (5th Ed. 2008)

Chapter 4: The Process of Legal Research Revisited

A. INTRODUCTION TO THIS SUPPLEMENT

In the main text of this Workbook, you have learned how to use many resources commonly relied on by individuals in the legal profession as they look for answers to important legal questions. In Assignment Sheets 1 through 5 you have put your hands on traditional hard copy resources as well as some popular online tools for finding and updating law. In addition, you have read **TIPS** and **WARNINGS** regarding those sources and others that you might use in the future.

This Supplement will provide you with a more focused opportunity to try your hand at additional techniques and sources used by legal researchers when they are working online. You will be given a new client and a new legal question to research in this Supplement, and you will complete Assignment Sheet 6 as you learn how to use online resources to find case law that will address that client's question. For convenience, Assignment Sheet 6 focuses exclusively on case law, but you will be able to generalize these same techniques in the future when you search for other kinds of information online.

As you have learned in your earlier lessons, Westlaw and LexisNexis are the principle providers of fee-based online legal research. In Assignment Sheet 6, you will have an opportunity to search for case law using each of these providers separately. When you have completed the Assignment Sheet assigned to you based on your earlier client, you can learn more by completing the other version of Assignment Sheet 6 that approaches Westlaw and LexisNexis in a different order. At the end of Assignment Sheet 6, you will also have the opportunity to be introduced to alternative fee-based and free online sources of legal information.

Online research tools, like all computer-related technology, change rapidly. The best way to become proficient at online research is to remain flexible and to look forward to innovation and change. At the end of Assignment Sheet 6 you will have a chance to explore online tutorials provided by LexisNexis and Westlaw. Frequent exploration of these tutorials will help keep you informed about the most current tools these services offer. Taking advantage of additional educational opportunities often available through local Bar Associations and other sources for Continuing Legal Education (CLE) credits in the future is another way to ensure that you remain competent and competitive in the rapidly changing world of legal research throughout your career.

B. THE INTELLIGENT USE OF ONLINE RESOURCES

In the 21st Century, lawyers and other legal researchers can obtain the legal information they need from a variety of sources that are available in any number of formats. The wide availability of competing sources of information is a positive thing for legal research, but requires competent researchers to adopt sophisticated strategies for choosing wisely among the resources available to them.

In developing sophisticated research strategies, it helps to visualize the answers to legal questions as being present in an information stream that you can join at many points of entry. Depending on your research goals, the particular role you play in the profession, and the depth of your familiarity with the general area of law involved, you can choose to enter this stream of information way up at the headwaters (where general information is available), or much further down river (where narrow and specific answers lie).

As an example, if you are responsible for thinking a legal problem through from beginning to end (if, for instance, you had a client who asked a very broad question such as "what are the financial consequences to me if I refuse to deliver goods on the contract I signed?"), you would want to be sure you had a broad sense of the legal tensions involved in the question as well as a solid sense of what kinds of primary law might control the result. Unless you were already very familiar with the relevant area of law, you would want to begin your search by gaining a "big picture" perspective. In such a case, you would be wise to begin with secondary sources (such as treatises, journal articles, or encyclopedias) that would introduce you to important concepts and key vocabulary terms with which to continue your search.

If, on the other hand, you were already an expert in contract law and had worked in the present jurisdiction for some time, you could enter the information stream further into the process because you would already have the big conceptual picture and would already know key vocabulary terms. You might, for example, already know that the question raised would be controlled by common law principles and might begin by looking for cases in your jurisdiction on point. Similarly, if you are working as part of a research team and have been asked to pull a specific statute or case for which you have already been given the citation, your task would be even more narrow and specific. There would be no reason to start with resources way up at the beginning of the stream of information. Instead, you could enter the citation itself in any number of available search engines (some for free, some for a cost) and pull up the information you need.

The temptation to begin a narrow search for legal information – metaphorically, to enter the information stream way downstream – is particularly strong for beginning researchers using online legal search engines for the first time. As you already know from general research you have done in other settings using search engines such as Yahoo or Google, any researcher can net an amazing amount of information simply by doing a whole language search of documents through an available search engine. The same thing is true in legal research. But the probability is high that such a general shotgun approach would be inefficient, unnecessarily expensive, and might well yield inaccurate results.

Rather than automatically launching word-driven searches based on intuition or guesswork, proficient legal researchers learn instead to weigh a number of factors when choosing a strategy and resources for conducting an intelligent search for legal information. In order, the factors to be considered are:

(1) **What type of information do I need to find?** (How much do I already know about the area of law that probably addresses this question; what are the likely primary sources of law that might determine the result; do I know the jurisdictions in which relevant law is likely to be found; am I interested only in the very current state of the law or would it be helpful to know how the law has evolved and whether related questions have been dealt with at an earlier time?)

(2) **What is my best available source for the type of information I've determined I need to find?** As you learned in the main Workbook, some information is only available in hard copy while other information is only available online. Where information is available in both formats, access in one might be easier and/or more affordable than access in another. Part of your role as an intelligent researcher will be to know your best sources and the best format in any given context. Becoming well-informed about competing resources and formats requires a daunting commitment of time and energy but nets high pay-offs for you, your employer, and your clients.

(3) **What are the costs of using various sources and when should economics influence the research choices I make?** The primary fee-based providers charge for the use of their services in a number of ways ranging from general use fees (such as the fee your law school pays for you to have access to Westlaw and LexisNexis) to fee-for-service arrangements that allow a researcher to pay for individual searches. In addition, wise researchers know that much of the information that is available for a fee is also available for free. Free services, however, often lack the kind of enhancements (such as the KeyCite or Shepard's features you explored in the Workbook) that are available for a fee and thus might, in the long run, not be the bargain they appear to be. Books, also, come at a cost in fees for storage space, cost of original acquisition of materials, and cost of maintaining supplementary updating materials. Once hard copy materials have been purchased, or where a researcher has access to an open library, there is no additional cost for on-going use of those materials. Finally, weighing the cost of research also requires consideration of the cost of your own time. Finding information conveniently online rather than driving an hour to a public-access library may well be a wise economic decision in some circumstances, or a very poor economic decision in others.

(4) Considering the materials available to me and the formats they are available in, are there ways I can minimize costs by finding an efficient way to approach the task? By thinking carefully ahead of time about the exact question (and related sub-questions) you are researching, thoughtfully identifying appropriate concepts and the words that describe them, choosing when to go online and when to work off-line, and using research enhancements such as West Key Numbers or LexisNexis Legal Topics to your advantage, you can save time and expense while ensuring thorough and accurate results using both hard copy and online materials.

C. TECHNIQUES USED TO ACCESS LEGAL INFORMATION ONLINE

1. Boolean Searching

Much of online legal research is based on Boolean logic. Boolean (pronounced "BOO-le-an") logic is named for English mathematician George Boole (1815-1864)[1]. Employing Boolean logic, legal researchers can capture meaning by placing words in relationship to each other using "core operators" like AND, OR, and NOT. Boolean searches retrieve documents that contain certain words but not others, or contain certain words in particular relationship to other words. Using these techniques, a researcher can search online with precision, describing a topic through words that reflect what it is and what it is not. For example, imagine that you wanted to employ Boolean logic to find a clip of a TV skit from an early Saturday Night Live Episode starring Chevy Chase but not including John Belushi. Assuming you had a search engine that could search a data base containing all clips from all TV shows, a Boolean search for a suitable skit might look like: "Saturday Night Live" AND "Chevy Chase" BUT NOT "John Belushi."

Similarly, legal researchers use search terms and Boolean connectors to find relevant documents from within the massive online databases of legal documents maintained by services such as Westlaw and LexisNexis. Some of the common Boolean connectors used by Westlaw and LexisNexis are the following:

AND   retrieves documents where both terms are included

OR   retrieves documents where either term is included[2]

/S   retrieves documents where the first term appears in the same sentence with the next

/P   retrieves documents where the first term appears in the same paragraph with the next

/n   retrieves documents where the first term appears within "n" words of the next

---

[1] For an interesting discussion of Boolean searching, see *Engate Inc. v. Esquire Deposition Svcs.*, 331 F. Supp. 2d 673, 688 n. 8 (N.C. Ill 2004).
[2] Note that Westlaw interprets a space between terms as "or."

" "	retrieves documents that include the exact phrase enclosed within the quotation marks
BUT NOT	retrieves documents that include one term without the other anywhere in the document (on Westlaw)
AND NOT	retrieves documents that include one term without the other anywhere in the document (on LexisNexis)
*	the universal character (e.g., *Sm*th* retrieves *Smith* and *Smyth*)
!	the root expander (e.g., *arbitrat!* retrieves *arbitration, arbitrator, arbitrate, arbitrating, etc.*)

Using these connectors (also called "operators"), a legal research seeking cases about rabies vaccination requirements for dogs might draft a Boolean search such as: **rabies /3 vaccination or shot /p dog**. This search would retrieve all cases in which the term *rabies* appears within three words of the term *vaccination* or *shot*, the combination of which would appear within the same paragraph as the word *dog*.

One final factor to consider about operators is that there is a default order set automatically in both Westlaw and LexisNexis that determines, by default, the order in which your choice of connectors is processed. The order in which operators are processed significantly impacts the results you will receive. You can over-ride the default order by adding parentheses to your Boolean search.

Westlaw and LexisNexis process connectors in the following order:

OR,
PROXIMINITY OPERATORS (w/s; w/p; w/25)
AND,
BUT NOT (in Westlaw) or AND NOT (in LexisNexis)

Turning back to the example above, the software will first find all cases that have either the word "vaccination" or the word "shot" in them. Next, the software will look at all of those cases to further narrow the search to those where the words "vaccination" or "shot" are within three words of "rabies." Finally, the software will narrow the search further to find cases that have the word "dog" within the same paragraph as the other terms as processed.

To alter that search to retrieve different results, you could add parentheses to control the order of operations: **(rabies /3 vaccination) or (shot /p dog)**. In this search, the software will look for cases that have the word "rabies" within three words of "vaccination" and will ALSO look for all cases in which the word "shot" is in the same paragraph as the word "dog." Thus, by adding parentheses to control the order of operations, you generally have a higher probability of netting more cases.

TIP: Both LexisNexis and Westlaw have menus readily available on the search screen to assist a legal researcher in choosing a Boolean connector.

TIP: Some words are so common that they are not helpful as search terms. Articles (the, an, a) and some conjunctions (and) are not searchable using Westlaw or LexisNexis. If such a word is necessary to your search, use quotation marks around it when you create your search. For example, "search and seizure" will find the entire phrase as written, including the word "and."

TIP: Some search terms will automatically provide results including variations of themselves, even without use of a universal character or a root expander. Westlaw and LexisNexis call such search terms "equivalents." For example, a Boolean search on Westlaw or LexisNexis for *E.P.A.* will retrieve *EPA* or *E.P.A.*, and a search for *fifty* will return cases including *fifty* or *50*. Similarly, a search for a singular noun (for example, *country*) will return results containing the singular noun and any regular plural (*countries*) or possessive (*country's*) forms.

TIP: Boolean searches may be further narrowed by using date restrictions and field or segment restrictions. Many databases, including Westlaw and LexisNexis, allow the researcher to impose date restrictions on the results of a search; these restrictions limit the cases retrieved to those from a particular time period chosen by the researcher. Field or segment restrictions allow a researcher to search for a term in a specific portion of a case such as the attorney names or the dissent. Restrictions appear in a separate box on the search screen in Westlaw and LexisNexis.

2. Other Methods of Searching

Using Natural Language
- Some databases, including those maintained by Westlaw and LexisNexis, allow legal researchers to search using a phrase, sentence, or list instead of conducting a Boolean search relying on Boolean terms and connectors. Using plain language is called natural language searching. Natural language searching can be helpful if you are unfamiliar with terms and connectors, or if you are uncertain of how key phrases relate to one another in the area you are researching. In the example from above, you might use the following natural language search: *must a pet owner vaccinate her dog against rabies*.

When you know the citation
- Both Westlaw and LexisNexis allow you to enter a citation and retrieve the document immediately. Using Westlaw, this function is titled "Find by Citation" and using LexisNexis it is titled "Get a Document." Both are available from the initial screen after entering your password.

When you know a party name
- If you know the name of the party to a case you want to view, of course you may use that name as part of a Boolean search. However, a Boolean search of the name will likely return more cases than the one you seek, since any later cases that cite your case will also be included. For example, a Boolean search for the party names *Hammack* and *Few* will return *Few v. Hammack*, but it also will return any case that cited *Few v. Hammack*. To remedy this problem, Westlaw has a specific type of search for case by party name. LexisNexis offers the same service as a variation of its Get a Document search. Additionally, many court websites contain opinions and can be searched for party name or docket number.

D. BEGINNING ASSIGNMENT SHEET 6

As you complete Assignment Sheet 6, you will have the opportunity to practice finding case law using Boolean searching, natural language searching, and by previously known document. To begin your work on this final Assignment Sheet, turn to the memo that corresponds to the client you have worked with in the main textbook:

• If you represent Client A, B, C, D, or E, turn to page 29 after reading your assigning memo to begin Assignment Sheet 6.

• If you represent Client F, G, H, I, or J, turn to page 45 after reading your assigning memo to begin Assignment Sheet 6.

MAP TO ACCOMPANY MEMOS 1-10, IMMEDIATELY FOLLOWING.

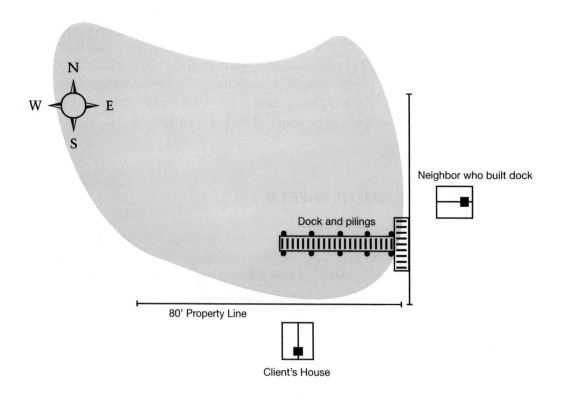

MARSHALL, STORY & ASSOCIATES
ATTORNEYS AND COUNSELORS AT LAW
SUITE 101, THE JUSTICE BUILDING

THE LITIGATION DIVISION

To: New Attorney
From: Assigning Partner
Re: Eric Arnold – File #03-2576 **(CLIENT A)**

Thank you for your good work for Mr. Arnold. He is very much enjoying his retired life on the farm, and he recently purchased a small house on a cove at a lake to use for fishing trips. He requires our assistance in a matter regarding this lake house.

Mr. Arnold's property has eighty feet of shoreline on the south side of the lake. His house looks out across the lake, facing directly north. Mr. Arnold's next-door neighbors immediately to his right at the lake are Ron and Teresa Jamison. The Jamisons' property and Mr. Arnold's property join at the southeast corner of the lake, with the Jamisons' house situated on the east side of the lake facing due west.

Last weekend, the Jamisons had a dock constructed to increase their enjoyment of their property. Unfortunately, the Jamisons' dock, which extends directly out from their property for a considerable distance, interferes significantly with Mr. Arnold's enjoyment of his property. The Jamisons' dock not only blocks Mr. Arnold's view of the lake, but a number of pylons supporting the dock are so close to his property that he is now prevented from ever building a dock of his own.*

Mr. Arnold wants to know whether the Jamison family is within its rights to place the dock and accompanying support pylons, or pillars, directly in front of his property. It has been many years since I last researched littoral rights. I need to know if there are any cases in our state addressing littoral rights, sometimes called riparian rights, to build a dock or pier into a lake. You may use online resources to conduct a brief search. I will speak with Mr. Arnold again next week, and I will share the results of your research with him then.

*See the accompanying map on page 8.

▶▶ **Turn Immediately to page 29 to begin your work
on Assignment Sheet 6**

MARSHALL, STORY & ASSOCIATES
ATTORNEYS AND COUNSELORS AT LAW
SUITE 101, THE JUSTICE BUILDING

THE LITIGATION DIVISION

To: New Attorney
From: Assigning Partner
Re: Project Hope – File #03-2575 **(CLIENT B)**

Thank you for the good work you have done on behalf of Project Hope. I know you must feel fulfilled as I do to see the school finally becoming a reality. Ms. Elizabeth Beattie is a Project Hope Board member who was so impressed with our work that she has decided to retain us in a property dispute regarding her lake house.

Several years ago, Ms. Beattie purchased a small cottage on a cove at the lake to use for weekend trips. Ms. Beattie's property has eighty feet of shoreline on the south side of the lake. Her house looks out across the lake, facing directly north.

Ms. Beattie's next-door neighbors immediately to his right are Jenni and Jon Lee. The Lees' property and Ms. Beattie's property join at the southeast corner of the lake, with the Lees' house situated on the east side of the lake facing due west.

Ms. Beattie and the Lees get along well, but this winter, while Ms. Beattie was away, the Lees had a dock constructed to increase their enjoyment of their property. Unfortunately, the Lees' dock, which extends directly out from their property for a considerable distance, interferes significantly with Ms. Beattie's enjoyment of her property. The Lees' dock not only blocks Ms. Beattie's view of the lake, but a number of pylons supporting the dock are so close to Ms. Beattie's property that she is now prevented from ever building a dock of her own.*

Ms. Beattie wants to know whether the Lee family is within its rights to place the dock and accompanying support pylons, or pillars, directly in front of her property. It has been many years since I last researched littoral rights. I need to know if there are any cases in our state addressing littoral rights, sometimes called riparian rights, to build a dock or pier into a lake. You may use online resources to conduct a brief search. I will speak with Ms. Beattie again next week after the Project Hope Board meeting, and I will share the results of your research with her then.

*See the accompanying map on page 8.

▶▶ Turn immediately to page 29 to begin your work
on Assignment Sheet 6

MARSHALL, STORY & ASSOCIATES
ATTORNEYS AND COUNSELORS AT LAW
SUITE 101, THE JUSTICE BUILDING

⚖

THE LITIGATION DIVISION

To: New Attorney
From: Assigning Partner
Re: Marjorie Morrison – File #21-2203 **(CLIENT C)**

Thank you for the research you completed for Ms. Morrison. Using the information you found, we were able to mediate a settlement for her and Mr. Thompson. In the months since the settlement, Ms. Morrison and her son have purchased a small lake cottage to use for family gatherings, and they would like our help in a new matter.

Ms. Morrison's property has eighty feet of shoreline on the south side of the lake. Ms. Morrison's house looks out across the lake, facing directly north. Ms. Morrison's next-door neighbors immediately to her right at the lake are David and Karen Scott. The Scotts' property and Ms. Morrison's property join at the southeast corner of the lake, with the Scotts' house situated on the east side of the lake, facing due west.

The families get along well, but last weekend the Scotts had a dock constructed to increase their enjoyment of their property. Unfortunately, the Scotts' dock, which extends directly out from their property for a considerable distance, interferes significantly with Ms. Morrison's enjoyment of her property. The Scotts' dock not only blocks Ms. Morrison's view of the lake, but a number of pylons supporting the dock are so close to her property that she is now prevented from ever building a dock of her own.*

Ms. Morrison wants to know whether the Scott family is within its rights to place the dock and accompanying support pylons, or pillars, directly in front of her property. It has been many years since I last researched littoral rights. I need to know if there are any cases in our state addressing littoral rights, sometimes called riparian rights, to build a dock or pier into a lake. You may use online resources to conduct a brief search. I will speak with Ms. Morrison again next week, and I will share the results of your research with her then.

*See the accompanying map on page 8.

▶▶ Turn immediately to page 29 to begin your work on Assignment Sheet 6

MARSHALL, STORY & ASSOCIATES
ATTORNEYS AND COUNSELORS AT LAW
SUITE 101, THE JUSTICE BUILDING

THE LITIGATION DIVISION

To: New Attorney
From: Assigning Partner
Re: Allen Field – File # 21-2204 **(CLIENT D)**

Thank you for the work you performed for Dr. Field. Because he has been so pleased with our work for him this year, he has referred a friend to us for assistance with a legal problem.

Dr. Field's neighbors, Joe and Pat Davison, own a small cottage on the lake that they use for weekend trips. The Davisons' property has eighty feet of shoreline on the south side of the lake. The Davisons' house looks out across the lake, facing directly north. Their next-door neighbors immediately to their right at the lake are Ellen and Cameron Parker. The Parkers' property and the Davisons' property join at the southeast corner of the lake, with the Parkers' house situated on the east side of the lake, facing due west.

The families have gotten along well for many years, but this winter, while the Davison family was away, the Parkers had a dock constructed to increase their enjoyment of their property. Unfortunately, the Parkers' dock, which extends directly out from their property for a considerable distance, interferes significantly with Mr. and Mrs. Davison's enjoyment of their property. The Parkers' dock not only blocks the Davisons' view of the lake, but a number of pylons supporting the dock are so close to their property that they are now prevented from ever building a dock of their own.*

Mr. and Mrs. Davison want to know whether the Parker family is within its rights to place the dock and accompanying support pylons, or pillars, directly in front of their property. It has been many years since I last researched littoral rights. I need to know if there are any cases in our state addressing littoral rights, sometimes called riparian rights, to build a dock or pier into a lake. You may use online resources to conduct a brief search. I will speak with Mr. Davison again next week, and I will share the results of your research with him then.

*See the accompanying map on page 8.

**▶▶ Turn immediately to page 29 to begin your work
on Assignment Sheet 6**

MARSHALL, STORY & ASSOCIATES
ATTORNEYS AND COUNSELORS AT LAW
SUITE 101, THE JUSTICE BUILDING

THE LITIGATION DIVISION

To: New Attorney
From: Assigning Partner
Re: Josh Ward – File #21-2205 **(CLIENT E)**

Thank you for the work you performed for Mr. Ward. Because he has been so pleased with our work for him this year, he has referred a friend to us. Mr. Ward's friend, Hector Lugo, owns a small cottage directly across the lake from Mr. Ward. Mr. Lugo uses his house as a writer's retreat on weekends and during the summer months. He has eighty feet of shoreline on the south side of the lake and his house looks out across the lake, facing directly north. Mr. Lugo's next-door neighbors immediately to his right at the lake are Ellen and Cameron Parker. His property and the Parkers' property join at the southeast corner of the lake, with the Parkers' house situated on the east side of the lake, facing due west.

Mr. Lugo has gotten along well with the Parkers have gotten along well for many years, but this winter, while Mr. Lugo was away, the Parkers had a dock constructed to increase their enjoyment of their property. Unfortunately, the Parkers' dock, which extends directly out from their property for a considerable distance, interferes significantly with Mr. Lugo's enjoyment of his property. The Parkers' dock not only blocks Mr. Lugo's view of the lake, but a number of pylons supporting the dock are so close to his property that he is now prevented from ever building a dock of his own.*

Mr. Lugo wants to know whether the Parker family is within its rights to place the dock and accompanying support pylons, or pillars, directly in front of his property. It has been many years since I last researched littoral rights. I need to know if there are any cases in our state addressing littoral rights, sometimes called riparian rights, to build a dock or pier into a lake. You may use online resources to conduct a brief search. I will speak with Mr. Lugo again next week, and I will share the results of your research with him then.

*See the accompanying map on page 8.

▶▶ **Turn immediately to page 29 to begin your work
on Assignment Sheet 6**

MARSHALL, STORY & ASSOCIATES
ATTORNEYS AND COUNSELORS AT LAW
SUITE 101, THE JUSTICE BUILDING

THE LITIGATION DIVISION

To: New Attorney
From: Assigning Partner
Re: Richard Roth – File #03-2578 **(CLIENT F)**

Thank you for the work you completed for Richard regarding his invention. We are optimistic that the outcome of his patent and defamation matters will be positive. Because he has been so pleased with our work for him this year, he has referred his parents to us for assistance with a legal problem.

Richard's parents, Sam and Melba Roth, own a small cottage on the lake. The Roth property has eighty feet of shoreline on the south side of the lake. The Roths' house looks out across the lake, facing directly north. Their next-door neighbors immediately to their right at the lake are Brian and Suzanne Gaff. The Roth property and the Gaff property join at the southeast corner of the lake, with the Gaffs' house situated on the east side of the lake, facing due west.

The families have gotten along well for many years, but this winter, while the Roth family was away, the Gaffs had a dock constructed to increase their enjoyment of their property. Unfortunately, the Gaffs' dock, which extends directly out from their property for a considerable distance, interferes significantly with the Mr. and Mrs. Roth's enjoyment of their property. The Gaffs' dock not only blocks their view of the lake, but a number of pylons supporting the dock are so close to their property that they are now prevented from ever building a dock of their own.*

Mr. and Mrs. Roth want to know whether the Gaff family is within its rights to place the dock and accompanying support pylons, or pillars, directly in front of their property. It has been many years since I last researched littoral rights. I need to know if there are any cases in our state addressing littoral rights, sometimes called riparian rights, to build a dock or pier into a lake. You may use online resources to conduct a brief search. I will speak with Mr. and Mrs. Roth again next week, and I will share the results of your research with them then.

*See the accompanying map on page 8.

▶▶ Turn immediately to page 45 to begin your work on Assignment Sheet 6

MARSHALL, STORY & ASSOCIATES
ATTORNEYS AND COUNSELORS AT LAW
SUITE 101, THE JUSTICE BUILDING

THE LITIGATION DIVISION

To: New Attorney
From: Assigning Partner
Re: Ana Martinez – File #03-2577 **(CLIENT G)**

Thank you for your work for Ana Martinez. She is grateful for our assistance and she certainly has learned to be more cautious in entering contracts. Because she has been so pleased with our work for her this year, she has referred her aunt to us for assistance with a legal problem.

Ms. Martinez's aunt, Lily Marguiles, purchased a small cottage on the lake to use for weekend trips. The property has several hundred feet of shoreline on the south side of the lake. Ms. Marguiles' house looks out across the lake, facing directly north. Ms. Marguiles' next-door neighbors immediately to her right at the lake are Jeff and Carolyn Sutton. The Suttons' property and Ms. Marguiles' property join at the southeast corner of the lake with the Suttons' house situated on the east side of the lake, facing due west.

The families get along well, but last weekend, the Suttons had a dock constructed to increase their enjoyment of their property. Unfortunately, the Suttons' dock, which extends directly out from their property for a considerable distance, interferes significantly with Ms. Marguiles' enjoyment of her property. The Suttons' dock not only blocks her view of the lake, but a number of pylons supporting the dock are so close to Ms. Marguiles' property that she is now prevented from ever building a dock of her own.*

Ms. Marguiles wants to know whether the Suttons are within their rights to place the dock and accompanying support pylons, or pillars, directly in front of her property. It has been many years since I last researched littoral rights. I need to know if there are any cases in our state addressing littoral rights, sometimes called riparian rights, to build a dock or pier into a lake. You may use online resources to conduct a brief search. I will speak with Ms. Marguiles again next week, and I will share the results of your research with her then.

*See the accompanying map on page 8.

**▶▶ Turn immediately to page 45 to begin your work
on Assignment Sheet 6**

MARSHALL, STORY & ASSOCIATES
ATTORNEYS AND COUNSELORS AT LAW
SUITE 101, THE JUSTICE BUILDING

THE LITIGATION DIVISION

To: New Attorney
From: Assigning Partner
Re: Christopher Smith – File #21-2206 (**CLIENT H**)

Thank you for your work for the Smiths. We are very hopeful that the mediation we have scheduled will satisfactorily resolve the matter. I am quite certain that Christopher will never again purchase a car without first obtaining a mechanic's inspection. The Smiths were so impressed with our work that they have decided to retain us in a property dispute regarding their lake house.

Several years ago, Mr. and Mrs. Smith purchased a small cottage on a cove at the lake to use for weekend trips. The Smiths' property has eighty feet of shoreline on the south side of the lake. The Smiths' house looks out across the lake, facing directly north.

Mr. and Mrs. Smith's next-door neighbors immediately to their right are Jaden and Brenna Reed. The Smiths' property and the Reeds' property join at the southeast corner of the lake, with the Reeds' house situated on the east side of the lake, facing due west.

The families have gotten along well for many years, but this winter, while the Smiths were away, the Reeds had a dock constructed to increase their enjoyment of their property. Unfortunately, the Reeds' dock, which extends directly out from their property for a considerable distance, interferes significantly with the Smiths' enjoyment of their property. The Reeds' dock not only blocks the Smiths' view of the lake, but a number of pylons supporting the dock are so close to the Smiths' property that they are now prevented from ever building a dock of their own.*

Mr. and Mrs. Smith want to know whether the Reed family is within its rights to place the dock and accompanying support pylons, or pillars, directly in front of their property. It has been many years since I last researched littoral rights. I need to know if there are any cases in our state addressing littoral rights, sometimes called riparian rights, to build a dock or pier into a lake. You may use online resources to conduct a brief search. I will speak with Mr. and Mrs. Smith again next week, and I will share the results of your research with them then.

*See the accompanying map on page 8.

▶▶ **Turn immediately to page 45 to begin your work
on Assignment Sheet 6**

MARSHALL, STORY & ASSOCIATES

ATTORNEYS AND COUNSELORS AT LAW
SUITE 101, THE JUSTICE BUILDING

THE LITIGATION DIVISION

To: New Attorney
From: Assigning Partner
Re: Carolyn Meyer – File #21-2207 **(CLIENT I)**

Thank you for your work on behalf of Carolyn Meyer. The Meyers were so impressed with our work that they have decided to retain us in a property dispute regarding their lake house.

Several years ago, Mr. and Mrs. Meyer purchased a small cottage on a cove at the lake to use for weekend trips. The Meyers' property has eighty feet of shoreline on the south side of the lake. The Meyers' house looks out across the lake, facing directly north.

The Meyers' next-door neighbors immediately to their right are Vanna and Tad Rohr. The Rohrs' property and the Meyers' property join at the southeast corner of the lake, with the Rohrs' house situated on the east side of the lake, facing due west.

The families have gotten along well for many years, but this winter, while the Meyers were away, the Rohrs had a dock constructed to increase their enjoyment of their property. Unfortunately, the Rohrs' dock, which extends directly out from their property for a considerable distance, interferes significantly with the Meyers' enjoyment of their property. The Rohrs' dock not only blocks their view of the lake, but a number of pylons supporting the dock are so close to the Meyers' property that they are now prevented from ever building a dock of their own.*

Mr. and Mrs. Meyer want to know whether the Rohr family is within its rights to place the dock and accompanying support pylons, or pillars, directly in front of their property. It has been many years since I last researched littoral rights. I need to know if there are any cases in our state addressing littoral rights, sometimes called riparian rights, to build a dock or pier into a lake. You may use online resources to conduct a brief search. I will speak with Mr. and Mrs. Meyer again next week, and I will share the results of your research with them then.

*See the accompanying map on page 8.

**▶▶ Turn immediately to page 45 to begin your work
on Assignment Sheet 6**

MARSHALL, STORY & ASSOCIATES
ATTORNEYS AND COUNSELORS AT LAW
SUITE 101, THE JUSTICE BUILDING

THE LITIGATION DIVISION

To: New Attorney
From: Assigning Partner
Re: Jeanne Martin – File #21-2208 **(CLIENT J)**

Thank you for your assistance with Ms. Martin's housing matter. Her family has been pleased with our work for her this year, and her aunt has come to us for assistance with a legal problem.

Ms. Martin's aunt, Emily Wood, purchased a small cottage on the lake to use for weekend trips. The property has eighty feet of shoreline on the south side of the lake. Ms. Wood's house looks out across the lake, facing directly north. Ms. Wood's next-door neighbors immediately to her right at the lake are Steve and Lisa Bailey. The Baileys' property and Ms. Wood's property join at the southeast corner of the lake, with the Baileys' house situated on the east side of the lake, facing due west.

The families get along well, but last weekend, the Baileys had a dock constructed to increase their enjoyment of their property. Unfortunately, the Baileys' dock, which extends directly out from their property for a considerable distance, interferes significantly with Ms. Wood's enjoyment of her property. The Baileys' dock not only blocks her view of the lake, but a number of pylons supporting the dock are so close to her property that she is now prevented from ever building a dock of her own.*

Ms. Wood wants to know whether the Bailey family is within its rights to place the dock and accompanying support pylons, or pillars, directly in front of her property. It has been many years since I last researched littoral rights. I need to know if there are any cases in our state addressing littoral rights, sometimes called riparian rights, to build a dock or pier into a lake. You may use online resources to conduct a brief search. I will speak with Ms. Wood again next week, and I will share the results of your research with her then.

*See the accompanying map on page 8.

▶▶ Turn immediately to page 45 to begin your work on Assignment Sheet 6

Assignment Sheet 6 *in Sequence of Assignments #1*
Accessing Information Online

Print Your Name:

Estimated Time
of Completion
(including recommended
background reading):
2.5 – 3.5 hrs.

**(Begin here ONLY if you represent Client A, B, C, D, or E.
Go to page 45 if you represent Client F, G, H, I, or J.)**

Background Information: As you have learned, the two most commonly used fee-based sources for conducting electronic research (computer assisted legal research or CALR) are Westlaw and LexisNexis. Westlaw and LexisNexis, divisions of legal publishers Thomson West and Reed Elsevier respectively, maintain computer databases containing the full texts of an extraordinary number of primary and secondary legal sources.

Westlaw and LexisNexis are similar (although each offers unique features with which you will want to become familiar), and you should practice until you are comfortable using both. Many of the techniques you use to conduct research on Westlaw and LexisNexis are the same tools you will use with other fee-based services as well. In Part A of this Assignment, you will learn how to search for common law using Boolean search techniques on Westlaw. In Part B of this Assignment, you will use LexisNexis to learn how to find a document when you already have a citation. You will also use LexisNexis to learn how to conduct a natural language search. When you are finished, if you have extra time, go to page 46 in this Supplement and you can try your hand at conducting a Boolean search on LexisNexis to find a case, and finding a document and conducting a natural language search on Westlaw.

> TIP: Although use of both Westlaw and LexisNexis is free to law students (but not free to their schools), fee structures vary widely in the private domain depending on the contractual arrangement an individual or entity has made with Westlaw or LexisNexis. For example, some contracts allow for payment by the minute, some allow for payment by the search, and some are based on a flat fee. Generally, under many contractual arrangements, the more restricted the database accessible under a particular contract, the lower the cost. Because fee structures vary so widely, it is always smart to find out how a service is billing your employer when you are researching in a new environment for the first time (for example, if you are a new summer associate at a law firm or agency). If you understand the fee structure, you can tailor your use of online time accordingly. Regardless of the particular fee structure, you will always save money if you organize and prepare your search before you sign on to Westlaw or LexisNexis.

> **TIP:** Westlaw and LexisNexis have account representatives who visit law schools to provide training for students. Check with your law librarian or research instructor, or email your representative using the links provided on westlaw.com and lexis.com, to find training sessions at your school. In addition, Westlaw and LexisNexis each have online tutorials that are available at no charge to you as a student. See page 44 in this Supplement. The more proficient you become at using these services (as well as the hard copy services taught in the main body of the textbook) now, the more valuable you become to your employer later.

What You Will Learn. By the end of this assignment, you will:

- Be able to formulate a Boolean search to find a case on Westlaw
- Be able to formulate a natural language search to find a case on LexisNexis
- Choose an appropriate database on Westlaw and LexisNexis
- Be able to expand or narrow your search to yield fewer or more cases
- Use Westlaw's "Research Trail" function and LexisNexis' "History" function to preserve your search for a limited number of days
- Use LexisNexis to find a known document
- Be able to identify additional free and fee-based online resources
- Know how to find helpful tutorials on Westlaw or LexisNexis

A. CONDUCTING A BOOLEAN SEARCH USING WESTLAW

Step 1: Organize your Search (Before Logging On!)

As with most of legal research, the first step is to organize. Organization is particularly important when using fee-based online services because time wasted is expensive.

    (a) State your issue/facts/topic
    (b) Choose your database
    (c) Create your search words and terms

> **TIP:** In certain states where large bodies of water are less common, or where otherwise directed by your instructor, you may choose to search for law in a neighboring state or in a database that combines state and federal cases in order to get the full benefit of this exercise.

(a) State your issue/facts/topic: The first step in organizing your search is to state your issue, facts, or topic to reflect the legal information you are seeking. For this assignment, an easy way to do this is by restating the question raised by your senior partner. Restate the question raised by your assignment in the following answer space.

Think of a few alternate ways to state the same question, then write them in the following answer space.

(b) Choose your database: Next, you need to decide which database is likely to have the law you seek (for example, state courts, federal courts, or a combination of both. Note that if you were searching for statutes or administrative regulations, rather than for case law, your database would be entirely different). Describe in five words or less below a possible common law database that you will be searching for your case law.

> **TIP:** The broader the database you select, the higher the online charge may be. Thus, you should focus your database as narrowly as possible without excluding relevant jurisdictions. For example, if you are researching a question of California state law, choose California state cases as opposed to a database containing all fifty states' courts – unless, of course, you are interested in how other state jurisdictions have treated the California question. In addition to generally being less expensive online, using a more narrow database also saves your own time by eliminating retrieval of unnecessary documents.

> **TIP:** Note that the Westlaw database name may not be worded exactly the same as your answer above, but if you have considered possible jurisdictional questions ahead of time, common sense will lead you to select the correct database when you are at the appropriate Westlaw screen.

(c) Create your search, choosing high pay-off words, terms, and phrases: Now, using your statement of the question from organizational step (a) above, and the description of Boolean searching from pp. 4-6 in Chapter 4 of this Supplement, isolate words and/or phrases that you think are key search terms. Modify these words, where appropriate, with the universal characters or root expanders described on pp. 4-5, and write them in the space below:

Decide which connectors to use to define the relationships between the terms, then write your final formulation of your search in the space below:

Step 2: Log On

Go to Westlaw.com and log on using the password issued by your law librarian or Westlaw representative.

> **TIP:** If you are taken to the lawschool.westlaw.com page, click the button that says "Research Now on Westlaw" on the left side of the screen. If you go straight to Westlaw, you will already be on the correct screen for beginning your research.

> **TIP:** The first time you enter your password, you will be asked if you would like the service to save (remember) your password so that you will not have to re-type the information every time you log on. If you are sharing a computer with other library or school patrons, you obviously do not want your password available for everyone to use. If, on the other hand, you are using your own computer, checking the save box will save you a little time in the future.

Step 3: Locate the database you selected

Click on the "Directory" tab at the top of the screen or on the "View Westlaw Directory" link at the left side of the screen and then use the links to the progressively more narrow database collections. Given the question in your Assigning Memo, your path likely will be to "U.S. State Materials," then to your state, and then to "Cases."

 TIP: As you become more experienced with Westlaw, you may learn the abbreviations for the databases and you may not need to use the directory in the future.

Step 4: Enter your Boolean search

In the box labeled "terms and connectors," enter the result of organization step (c) (from Step 1) above. If you do not find any cases with your first search, click "Edit search" at the top left of the screen, modify the terms a bit, and search again.

 TIP: Westlaw's "Research Trail" function saves your searches for fourteen days. Click the "Research Trail" button at the top right of the screen to view your previous searches. Westlaw allows attorneys to re-access results for no additional charge until 2 a.m. the next day.

 TIP: If you aren't finding any cases:

(1) Broaden your results by eliminating terms that may be overly restricting the search or by expanding your database. You may also increase results by using the "OR" connector, by eliminating restricting connectors, and/or by adding parentheses to manage the order in which connectors are processed.

(2) Get help from others. If you enter several alternative searches without retrieving any cases, ask for help from a law librarian, your professor, or a teaching assistant. A last resort help option is to call the Westlaw reference attorneys at 1-800-850-WEST. These lawyers can help get you in the ballpark with your search. Live online help is also available under the help menu at the top of the screen.

TIP: If you are finding too many cases:

(1) Further narrow your results. Click the words "Locate in Result" found at the center of the page that lists your results. This feature allows you to add additional search terms that can narrow your research, and then searches the cases you already found for cases that *also* contain the new terms.

(2) Use date or field restrictions. You may limit your results using the Connectors/Expanders box, the Fields box, or the Date Restriction boxes located below the Terms and Connectors box. Clicking on the titles of these boxes gives you more information about these functions.

Step 5: Review the results of your search

Initially you will see a list of cases with hyperlinks that can take you to the full opinions. Select one opinion that seems as though it might be relevant to the question and click on the case caption to see the full case. Once you are on the screen that has the full opinion, use the "Term" arrow at the bottom of the screen to jump through the document to find your search terms. Recognizing that using this "term arrow" is a way of skimming (not thoroughly reading) a case, does the case still seem relevant (and, hence, worth reading carefully if you were working on a real case)? You may also use the "Doc" arrows to jump from case to case if the first case you view does not appear relevant.

To show your professor at least one case you found, please print a case (or the first three pages of a case) you have retrieved that is relevant to the partner's question. Using the buttons at the top of the screen, you may print to an attached printer, a stand-alone printer, or you may download the case to a disk or a flash drive for later printing. **ATTACH THE THREE PAGES TO THIS ASSIGNMENT.**

Step 6: Update the Case

As you learned in the main Workbook, Westlaw provides KeyCite, a case law and statutes citator that notifies you of potentially important information about your case. West's staff lawyers assign "status icons" to each case that will appear as one of the following graphics in the upper left-hand corner of the first screen of a case: A red flag sign indicates a negative case treatment in the chain of citing cases (for example, reversed or abrogated); a yellow flag indicates a possible negative treatment in the chain of citing cases (for example, opinion criticized); capital letter "H" means that the case has subsequent history; capital letter "C" means there are cases or other sources that cite your case. Cases that West's staff attorneys have not identified as having been cited in later opinions do not have a signal at all.

An icon, if assigned, will appear next to the case name in the results list and also to the left of the case text when you are viewing a case. You can access the KeyCite feature by clicking on a status icon anywhere it appears on the screen, or by clicking links that appear to the left of the case you are reading.

TIP: In addition to accessing KeyCite by clicking on an icon in a case you have retrieved, you can also access KeyCite directly, without first performing a search, by clicking on the "KeyCite" tab at the top of any Westlaw screen.

BEWARE: Regardless of the color or presence of flags, a competent researcher reviews all cases that cite his or her original case. Do not make a judgment concerning a case's current validity based upon the presence or absence of flags alone. The flags reflect West's staff attorneys' opinions and are provided merely as tools for you in your research; they do not substitute for your own judgment about the meaning or significance of a case's treatment in subsequent cases. The only way to exercise your judgment about the import of a case is to read the relevant case on your own. The flags can help you predict whether a particular case is one that you should investigate further.

READING TIP: Reading specialists are studying the effect of reading online, noting that reading material from a screen is a different physical and mental process than reading in traditional hard copy materials. While this is a new field of research, the bottom line is that, for most people, it is useful to download and print a copy of important material to read in hard copy form. Also, under some (but not all) fee arrangements, reading while online costs money while downloading material to read later does not.

TIP: KeyCite groups cases using "depth of treatment" stars. The presence of four stars indicates that your case is thoroughly discussed in the citing case; fewer stars indicates less extensive discussion.

In the space provided below, write the citation to one case that cites your case. If no cases cite your case, note that fact as well.

Has your case generated any negative history? "Negative history" means that the case has been overruled or modified in a negative manner on appeal and/or been otherwise distinguished or discussed unfavorably in a subsequent, unrelated case. In the space below, briefly (in one or two sentences) explain what cues have led you to predict that your case may or may not have negative history.

Has your case generated any positive history? "Positive history" means the case has been upheld on appeal and/or otherwise been favorably applied or discussed in a subsequent, unrelated case. In the space below, briefly (in one or two sentences) explain what cues have led you to predict that your case may or may not have positive history.

In the interest of time, we are not asking you to read either the original case you found or any of the cases indicating negative or positive history. If this were a real-life research project, why should you read those cases? Are there any other cases that you might also read?

Step 7: Print Your Research Trail

Click on "Research Trail" at the top right of the any Westlaw screen. When your research trail appears, click on "Download Trail" at the top right of the list. Click "Download" and then select "Print" from the File menu. **ATTACH YOUR RESEARCH TRAIL TO THIS PAGE OF THIS ASSIGNMENT.**

When you are finished, click "Sign Off" at the top right of the screen.

B. USING LEXISNEXIS TO LOCATE A KNOWN DOCUMENT

Background Information: When conducting research in the "real world," you are unlikely to switch between LexisNexis and Westlaw midway through a project as we are having you do here. We structure this Assignment this way in order to maximize your exposure to both services with the least repetition of work on your part. For this portion of your Online Assignment, you will take the citation of one of the cases you found when updating your original case in Part A (or you may use the original case itself if that case was not cited in a later case) and you will learn how to use the "Get a Document" feature on LexisNexis to retrieve it. On Westlaw, a similar document retrieving feature is called "Find by Citation."

Step 1: Organize your Search (Before Logging On!)

As with most of legal research, the first step is to organize. Look back to Step 6 of section A on page 34 of this Supplement. Write the citation of the case you found for that question in the following space (if your case had never been cited, use your original case from Step 5, page 34).

> **TIP:** To use "Get a Document," you will not have to select a database. LexisNexis automatically searches the appropriate database to retrieve the requested document.

Step 2: Log On

Go to Lexis.com and log on using the password issued by your law librarian or LexisNexis representative.

> **TIP:** The first time you log on with LexisNexis, the computer will ask you to create a unique user ID and password to replace the one issued to you originally by LexisNexis. Also, the first time you enter your password, you may be asked if you would like the service to save (remember) your password so that you will not have to re-type the information every time you log on. If you are sharing a computer with other library or school patrons, you obviously do not want your password available for everyone to use. If, on the other hand, you are using your own computer, checking the save box will save you a little time in the future.

Step 3: Choose "Get a Document" and "By Citation"

The "Get a Document" tab is near the top of the screen and appears like a file folder tab. Click on "Get a Document" to access that feature now.

TIP: "Get a Document" allows you to choose to retrieve a case by its citation, by a party's name, or by the docket number of the case.

Step 4: Enter the case citation into the search field

In the space provided by the "Get a Document" function, enter the citation to the case you are retrieving. When the case appears on the screen, print the case (or the first three pages of the case) and attach it to this page of this Assignment.

 TIP: Using links located at the upper right of the screen, you may print to an attached printer, a stand-alone printer, or you may download the case to a disk or a flash drive for later printing.

Step 5: Update the Case

As you learned in the main body of this Workbook, LexisNexis provides access to Shepard's Citation Service for updating. The Shepard's signals, which are shorthand indicators of possible treatment of your case by later cases, appear as icons next to the caption on the first screen of a case. For example, a red stop sign indicates a negative case treatment (such as reversal); a yellow triangle indicates a possible negative treatment (such as criticized or modified); and a green diamond with a plus sign (+) in the middle indicates positive treatment (such as followed or affirmed).

BEWARE: Regardless of the color or presence of a signal icon, a competent researcher reviews the citing cases. Do not make a judgment concerning a case's validity based upon the icons alone. The icons represent LexisNexis' staff attorneys' opinions and are provided merely as tools for you in your research; they do not substitute for your own judgment about the meaning or significance of a case's treatment in subsequent cases.

Update your research by clicking on the signal icon if one appears on the first page of the case you have retrieved, by clicking on the word "Shepardize" in the top center of the screen, or by clicking on the "Shepard's" tab at the top left of the screen.

 TIP: Notice the legend reminding you of the meaning of all signal icons at the very bottom of the Shepard's screen.

Has this case generated any negative history? "Negative history" means that the case has been overruled or modified in a negative manner on appeal and/or has been otherwise distinguished or discussed unfavorably in a subsequent, unrelated case. Briefly (in one or two sentences) explain what research cues have led you to conclude that your case does or does not have negative history.

Has this case generated any positive history? "Positive history" means the case has been upheld on appeal and/or otherwise been favorably applied or discussed in a subsequent, unrelated case. Briefly (in one or two sentences) explain what cues have led you to conclude that your case does or does not have any positive history.

Do NOT sign off yet. Stay on the Shepard's page to complete Part C below.

C. CONDUCTING A NATURAL LANGUAGE SEARCH USING LEXISNEXIS

Step 1: Formulate your search

Turn back to page 32 in Section A of this Assignment. Beginning with your Boolean search terms from your Westlaw exercise, create a new phrase in plain language that will reflect the partner's question. Write this new phrase or sentence in the space below.

Step 2: Select your Database and the Natural Language function

From the Shepard's page you were using when you completed Part B of this Assignment, click on the tab on the top left corner of the screen that says "Search." Use the links under "Look for a Source" to narrow your database to the one that most closely matches the database you used in the Westlaw exercise. Your path likely will be to "States Legal - U.S.," then to your particular state.

Once you see the "Enter Search Terms" box, click the circle next to Natural Language at the top of the box.

Step 3: Enter your search phrase in the Search Terms box

Type your phrase into the Enter Search Terms box and press enter.
Did your natural language search find cases? _____

Which method (Natural Language or Boolean) seems to produce the best results for this particular research question? Why do you think so?

Step 4: View and Print your History

LexisNexis' "History" function (at the top right of the screen) saves your searches and allows you to go back to the results later. Original results can be viewed again at no extra charge until 2 a.m. the next day, and search histories are saved for thirty days.

From the History screen, click "View Printable History" and print your LexisNexis history from this session. **ATTACH A COPY OF THAT SEARCH HISTORY TO THIS PAGE OF THIS ASSIGNMENT.**

Step 5: Sign Off

Remember to click on the "Sign Off" button when you have completed this part of your Assignment.

D. DISCOVERING OTHER ELECTRONIC RESOURCES

Background Information: The presence of the Internet has changed the way all of us access information, and its impact on legal research is just as great. As with all internet research, accessing legal information requires the use of caution and common sense in discerning the accuracy and reliability of the information you gather online. Consider your source and how frequently information is updated before depending on it either as a useful tool to gather background information before launching a search on a fee-based service, or as a source of primary law itself.

Following is an illustrative listing of some of the many reliable internet sites maintained by various entities that can be used to conduct legal research.

> **TIP:** In addition to these sites, a diligent researcher can uncover many other sources including blogs associated with legal scholars, politicians, and journalists, as well as local community websites containing information online ranging from tax and real property records to the full texts of local ordinances and regulations.

Subscription Sites (Sites requiring users to pay a fee for service)

- LexisNexis (www.lexis.com)

- Westlaw (www.westlaw.com)

- Loislaw (www.loislaw.com)

- VersusLaw (www.versuslaw.com)

- Hein-OnLine (http://heinonline.org)

- Casemaker (offered on many state bar association websites for association members)

> **TIP:** Many of the subscription sites have agreements with law schools that provide law students free access. Ask your law librarian or instructor for more information.

Compilation Sites (Sites providing links to other internet sources of legal information)

- The Legal Information Institute at Cornell Law School (www.law.cornell.edu)

- Washburn University School of Law (www.washlaw.edu)

- Findlaw (www.findlaw.com)

Court and Government Sites[3] (Sites provided by various government offices and courts. In addition to these sites of general interest, many state and federal administrative agencies and local governments maintain web pages with legal information.)

- State websites (maintained independently by each state) (www.state.___ .us)
  (insert state's postal abbreviation in place of blank)

- Supreme Court of the United States (www.supremecourtus.gov)

- Federal Courts (www.uscourts.gov)

- Individual Circuit Courts (www.ca___.uscourts.gov)
  (insert Circuit number 1-11 in place of blank)

- DC Circuit Court: (www.cadc.uscourts.gov)

- Federal Circuit: (www.fedcir.gov)

- Federal Legislative Information – THOMAS – including bills and full text of Congressional documents (http://thomas.loc.gov)

- Government Printing Office – U.S. Code, Code of Federal Regulations, Federal Register, Congressional Record, mid-1990's to present (www.gpoaccess.gov)

    Step 1: Select and visit a website that is appealing to you from the list set out above.

    Step 2: In the space below, or on a separate piece of paper attached to this page of this Assignment, describe the primary features of the site you have discovered.

---

[3] In addition to these truly free government websites, PACER (Public Access to Court Electronic Records) is available to the public at http://pacer.psc.uscourts.gov. From PACER, researchers can obtain case and docket information from most Federal Appellate, District, and Bankruptcy courts, and from the U.S. Party/Case Index. There is a per-page charge to view documents, and a password is required.

Step 3: In what way might you (or someone to whom you would recommend the site) use this site in the future?

E. USING ONLINE TUTORIALS

Background Information: Becoming confident and competent in your use of LexisNexis and Westlaw takes time (and energy), and is an ongoing, lifetime challenge. To help keep subscribers abreast of the multitude of constantly changing resources and functions available through their services, both Westlaw and LexisNexis provide sophisticated online tutorials.

Step 1: Choose *either* Westlaw *or* LexisNexis, and sign on.

Step 2: Locate a link on the service you have selected to its online tutorials. Note that you may (or may not) need to go to the "for law students" website for either Westlaw or LexisNexis to locate useful tutorials. Tutorials generally can be found using the "Help" menu or the "Site map" link.

Step 3: Select a tutorial on a topic that is of interest to you and complete that tutorial now. In the space below, or on a separate sheet of paper attached to this page of this Assignment, describe the tutorial and how it might be valuable to another student.

Congratulations! You have learned to perform basic online research using Westlaw and LexisNexis, you have become familiar with the wide variety of online resources available to a legal researcher, and you have learned how to access tutorials online for either Westlaw or LexisNexis. If you want additional practice using Westlaw or LexisNexis, turn to page 45 of this Supplement for another chance to try your skills.

Please note your actual time of completion (including background reading): _____ *hrs.*

Assignment Sheet 6 *in Sequence of Assignments #2* **Accessing Information Online**	Estimated Time of Completion (including recommended background reading): 2.5 – 4.0 hrs.
Print Your Name:	

**(Begin here ONLY if you represent Client F, G, H, I, or J.
Go to page 29 if you represent Client A, B, C, D, or E.)**

Background Information: As you have learned, the two most commonly used fee-based sources for conducting electronic research (computer assisted legal research or CALR) are Westlaw and LexisNexis. Westlaw and LexisNexis, divisions of legal publishers Thomson West and Reed Elsevier respectively, maintain computer databases containing the full texts of an extraordinary number of primary and secondary legal sources. Researchers use either Boolean search strategies or natural language searching to retrieve documents from these (and similar) databases.

Westlaw and LexisNexis are similar (although each offers unique features with which you will want to become familiar), and you should practice until you are comfortable using both. Many of the techniques you use to conduct research on Westlaw and LexisNexis are the same tools you will use with other fee-based services as well. In Part A of this Assignment, you will learn how to search for common law using Boolean search techniques on LexisNexis. In Part B of this Assignment, you will use Westlaw to learn how to find a document when you already have a citation. You will also use Westlaw to learn how to conduct a natural language search. When you are finished, if you have extra time, go to page 30 in this Supplement and you can try your hand at conducting a Boolean search on Westlaw to find a case, and finding a document and conducting a natural language search on LexisNexis.

TIP: Although use of both Westlaw and LexisNexis is free to law students (but not free to their schools), fee structures vary widely in the private domain depending on the contractual arrangement an individual or entity has made with Westlaw or LexisNexis. For example, some contracts allow for payment by the minute, some allow for payment by the search, and some are based on a flat fee. Generally, in either case, the more restricted the database accessible under a particular contract, the lower the cost. Because fee structures vary so widely, it is always smart to find out how a service is billing your employer when you are researching in a new environment for the first time (for example, if you are a new summer associate at a law firm or agency). If you understand the fee structure, you can tailor your use of online time accordingly. Regardless of the particular fee structure, you will always save money if you organize and prepare your search before you sign on to Westlaw or LexisNexis.

TIP: Westlaw and LexisNexis have account representatives who visit law schools to provide training for students. Check with your law librarian or research instructor, or email your representative using the links provided on westlaw.com and lexis.com, to find training sessions at your school. In addition, Westlaw and LexisNexis each have online tutorials that are available at no charge to you as a student. See page 59 in this supplement. The more proficient you become at using these services (as well as the hard copy services taught in the main body of the textbook) now, the more valuable you become to your employer later.

What You Will Learn. By the end of this assignment, you will:

- Be able to formulate a Boolean search to find a case on LexisNexis
- Be able to formulate a natural language search to find a case on Westlaw
- Choose an appropriate database on Westlaw and LexisNexis
- Be able to expand or narrow your search to yield fewer or more cases
- Use Westlaw's "Research Trail" function and LexisNexis' "History" function to preserve your search for a limited number of days
- Use Westlaw to find a known document
- Be able to identify additional free and fee-based online resources
- Know how to find helpful tutorials on Westlaw or LexisNexis

A. CONDUCTING A BOOLEAN SEARCH USING LEXISNEXIS

Step 1: Organize your Search (Before Logging On!)

As with most of legal research, the first step is to organize. Organization is particularly important when using fee-based CALR because time wasted is expensive.

      (a) **State your issue/facts/topic**
      (b) **Choose your database**
      (c) **Create your search words and terms**

TIP: In certain states where large bodies of water are less common, or where otherwise directed by your instructor, you may choose to search for law in a neighboring state or in a database that combines state and federal cases in order to get the full benefit of this exercise.

(a) State your issue/facts/topic: The first step in organizing your search is to state your issue, facts, or topic to reflect the legal information you are seeking. For this assignment, an easy way to do this is by restating the question raised by your senior partner. Restate the question raised by your assignment in the following answer space.

Think of a few alternate ways to state the same question, then write them in the following answer space.

(b) Choose your database: Next, you need to decide which database is likely to have the law you seek (for example, state courts, federal courts, or a combination of both. Note that if you were searching for statutes or administrative regulations, rather than for case law, your database would be entirely different.). Describe in five words or less below a possible common law database that you will be searching for your case law.

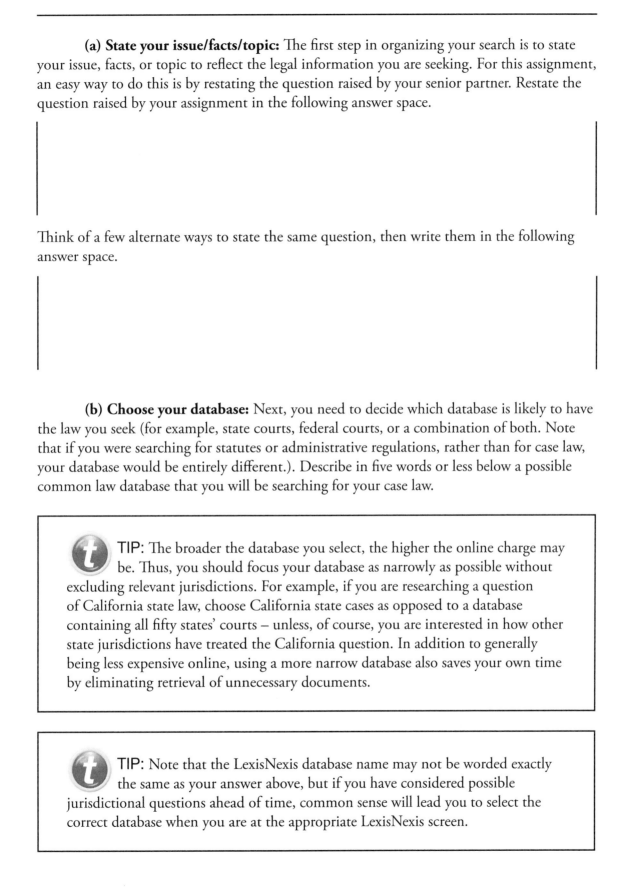

> **TIP:** The broader the database you select, the higher the online charge may be. Thus, you should focus your database as narrowly as possible without excluding relevant jurisdictions. For example, if you are researching a question of California state law, choose California state cases as opposed to a database containing all fifty states' courts – unless, of course, you are interested in how other state jurisdictions have treated the California question. In addition to generally being less expensive online, using a more narrow database also saves your own time by eliminating retrieval of unnecessary documents.

> **TIP:** Note that the LexisNexis database name may not be worded exactly the same as your answer above, but if you have considered possible jurisdictional questions ahead of time, common sense will lead you to select the correct database when you are at the appropriate LexisNexis screen.

(c) Create your search, using high pay-off words, terms, and phrases: Now, using your statement of the question from organizational step (a) above, and the description of Boolean searching from pp. 4-6 in Chapter 4 of this Supplement, isolate words and/or phrases that you think are key search terms. Modify these words, where appropriate, with the universal characters or root expanders described on pp. 4-5, and write them in the space below.

Decide which connectors to use to define the relationships between the terms, then write your final formulation of your search in the space below.

Step 2: Log On

Go to Lexis.com and log on using the password issued by your law librarian or LexisNexis representative.

 TIP: The first time you log on with LexisNexis, the computer will ask you to create a unique user ID and password to replace the one issued to you originally by LexisNexis. Also, the first time you enter your password, you may be asked if you would like the service to save (remember) your password so that you will not have to re-type the information every time you log on. If you are sharing a computer with other library or school patrons, you obviously do not want your password available for everyone to use. If, on the other hand, you are using your own computer, checking the save box will save you a little time in the future.

Step 3: Locate the database you selected

If you are not automatically routed to the page including the "Look for a Source" screen when you log on to Lexis.com, click on the tab on the top left of the screen that says "Search." Then, use the links under "Look for a Source" to progressively narrow your database. Given the question in your Assigning Memo, your path likely will be to "States Legal - U.S.," then to your particular state.

 TIP: As you become more experienced with LexisNexis, you may learn the abbreviations for the databases and you may not need to use the directory.

Step 4: Enter your Boolean search

In the box labeled "Enter Search Terms," enter the result of organization step (c) (from Step 1) above. If you do not find any cases with your first search, click "Edit search" at the top left of the screen, modify the terms a bit, and search again.

 TIP: LexisNexis' "History" function saves your searches for thirty days. Click the "History" button at the top right of the screen to view your previous searches and to re-access results for no additional charge until 2 a.m. the next day.

 TIP: If you aren't finding any cases:

(1) Broaden your results by eliminating terms that may be overly restricting the search or by expanding your database. You may also increase results by using the "OR" connector, by eliminating more restrictive connectors, and/or by adding parentheses to manage the order in which connectors are processed.

(2) Get help from others. If you enter several alternative searches without retrieving any cases, ask for help from a law librarian, your professor, or a teaching assistant. A last resort help option is to call the LexisNexis reference attorneys at 1-800-45-LEXIS. These lawyers can help get you in the ballpark with your search. Live online help is also available by clicking the "Live Support" button at the top of the screen.

TIP: If you are finding too many cases:

(1) Focus your results. Click the words "Focus Options" found at the center of the page that lists your results. This feature allows you to add additional search terms that can narrow your research, and then searches the cases you already found for cases that *also* contain the new terms.

(2) Use date or segment restrictions. You may limit your results using the Restrict by Segment box or the Restrict by Date box located below the Enter Search Terms box. Clicking on the titles of these boxes gives you more information about these functions.

Step 5: Review the results

Initially you will see a list of cases with hyperlinks that can take you to the full opinions. Select one opinion that seems as though it might be relevant to the question and click on the case caption to see the full case. Once you are on the screen that has the full opinion, use the "Term" arrow at the bottom of the screen to jump through the document to find your search terms. Recognizing that using this "term arrow" is a way of skimming (not thoroughly reading) a case, does the case still seem relevant (and, hence, worth reading carefully if you were working on a real case)? You may also use the "Doc" arrows to jump from case to case if the first case you view does not appear relevant.

To show your professor at least one case you found, please print a case (or the first three pages of a case) you have retrieved that is relevant to the partner's question. Using the buttons at the top of the screen, you may print to an attached printer, a stand-alone printer, or you may download the case to a disk or a flash drive for later printing. **ATTACH THE THREE PAGES TO THIS ASSIGNMENT.**

Step 6: Update the Case

As you learned in the main Workbook, LexisNexis provides access to Shepard's Citation Service for updating. The Shepard's signals, which are shorthand indicators of possible treatment of your case by later cases, appear as icons next to the caption on the first screen of a case. For example, a red stop sign indicates a negative case treatment (such as reversal); a yellow triangle indicates a possible negative treatment (such as criticized or modified); and a green diamond with a plus sign (+) in the middle indicates positive treatment (such as followed or affirmed).

 BEWARE: Regardless of the color or presence of a signal icon, a competent researcher reviews the citing cases. Do not make a judgment concerning a case's validity based upon the icons alone. The icons represent LexisNexis' staff attorneys' opinions and are provided merely as tools for you in your research; they do not substitute for your own judgment about the meaning or significance of a case's treatment in subsequent cases. The only way to exercise your judgment about the import of a case is to read the relevant case on your own. The icons can help you predict whether a particular case is one that you should investigate further.

TIP: Notice the legend reminding you of the meaning of all signal icons at the very bottom of the Shepard's screen.

READING TIP: Reading specialists are studying the effect of reading online, noting that reading material from a screen is a different physical and mental process than reading in traditional hard copy materials. While this is a new field of research, the bottom line is that, for most people, it is useful to download and print a copy of important material to read in hard copy form. Also, under some (but not all) fee arrangements, reading while online costs money while downloading material to read later does not.

 TIP: Shepard's organizes citing authority by jurisdiction.

To access Shepard's, click on the signal icon anywhere you see it. The icon appears next to the case name in the results list and also to the left of the case name when you are viewing a case. Alternatively, you can click the word "Shepardize" in the center top portion of the screen or click the tab labeled "Shepard's" at the very top of the screen.

TIP: You can access Shepard's directly, without first performing a search, using the tab at the top of the screen.

Write the citation of one case that cites your case in the space below. If no cases cite your case, note that as well.

Has your case generated any negative history? "Negative history" means that the case has been overruled or modified in a negative manner on appeal and/or been otherwise distinguished or discussed unfavorably in a subsequent, unrelated case. In the space below, briefly (in one or two sentences) explain what cues have led you to predict that your case may or may not have negative history.

Has your case generated any positive history? "Positive history" means the case has been upheld on appeal and/or otherwise been favorably applied or discussed in a subsequent, unrelated case. In the space below, briefly (in one or two sentences) explain what cues have led you to predict that your case may or may not have positive history.

In the interest of time, we are not asking you to read either the original case you found or any of the cases indicating negative or positive history. If this were a real-life research project, why should you read those cases? Are there any other cases that you might also read?

Step 7: Print your search history

LexisNexis' "History" function (at the top right of the screen) saves your searches and allows you to go back to the results later. Original results can be viewed again at no extra charge until 2 a.m. the next day, and search histories are saved for thirty days.

From the history screen, click "View Printable History" and print your LexisNexis history from this session. **ATTACH A COPY OF THAT SEARCH HISTORY TO THIS PAGE OF THIS ASSIGNMENT.**

When you are finished, log off by clicking "Sign Off" at the top right of the screen.

B. USING WESTLAW TO LOCATE A KNOWN DOCUMENT

Background Information: When conducting research in the "real world," you are unlikely to switch between LexisNexis and Westlaw midway through a project as we are having you do here. We structure this Assignment this way in order to maximize your exposure to both services with the least repetition of work on your part. For this portion of your Online Assignment, you will take the citation of one of the cases you found when updating your original case in Part A (or you may use the original case itself if that case was not cited in a later case) and you will learn how to use the "Find by Citation" feature on Westlaw to retrieve it. On LexisNexis, a similar document retrieving feature is called "Get a Document."

Step 1: Organize your Search (Before Logging On!)

As with most of legal research, the first step is to organize. Look back to Step 6 of section A on page 50 of this Supplement. Write the citation of the case you found for that question in the following space (if your case had never been cited, use your original case from Step 5, page 50).

TIP: To use Find by Citation you will not have to select a database. Westlaw automatically searches the appropriate database to retrieve the requested document.

Step 2: Log On

Go to Westlaw.com and log on using the password issued by your law librarian or Westlaw representative.

TIP: If you are taken to the lawschool.westlaw.com page, click the button that says "Research Now on Westlaw" on the left side of the screen. If you go straight to Westlaw, you will already be on the correct screen for beginning your research.

TIP: The first time you enter your password, you will be asked if you would like the service to save (remember) your password so that you will not have to re-type the information every time you log on. If you are sharing a computer with other library or school patrons, you obviously do not want your password available for everyone to use. If, on the other hand, you are using your own computer, checking the save box will save you a little time in the future.

Step 3: Enter the case citation into the Find by Citation search field

The "Find by Citation" box is near the top left of the screen. Enter the case citation into the search field. When the case appears on the screen, print the case (or the first three pages of the case) and attach it to this page of this Assignment.

> **TIP:** Using the buttons at the top of the screen, you may print to an attached printer, a stand-alone printer, or you may download the case to a disk or a flash drive for later printing.

Step 4: Update the Case

As you learned in the main Workbook, Westlaw provides KeyCite, a case law and statutes citator that notifies you of potentially important information about your case. West's staff lawyers assign "status icons" to each case that will appear as one of the following graphics in the upper left-hand corner of the first screen of a case: A red flag sign indicates a negative case treatment in the chain of citing cases (for example, reversed or abrogated); a yellow flag indicates a possible negative treatment in the chain of citing cases (for example, opinion criticized); capital letter "H" means that the case has subsequent history; capital letter "C" means there are cases or other sources that cite your case. Cases that have not been cited in later opinions do not have a signal at all.

A status icon, if assigned, will appear next to the case name in the results list and also to the left of the case text when you are viewing a case. You can access the KeyCite feature by clicking on a status icon anywhere it appears on the screen, or by clicking links that appear to the left of the case you are reading.

> **TIP:** In addition to accessing KeyCite by clicking on an icon in a case you have retrieved, you can also access KeyCite directly, without first performing a search, by clicking on the "KeyCite" tab at the top of any Westlaw screen.

> **BEWARE:** Regardless of the color or presence of a status icon, a competent researcher reviews all cases that cite his or her original case. Do not make a judgment concerning a case's current validity based upon the presence or absence of icons alone. The icons reflect West's staff attorneys' opinions and are provided merely as tools for you in your research; they do not substitute for your own judgment about the meaning or significance of a case's treatment in subsequent cases.

Has this case generated any negative history? As you will recall, "negative history" means that the case has been overruled or modified in a negative manner on appeal and/or been otherwise distinguished or discussed unfavorably in a subsequent, unrelated case. Briefly (in one or two sentences) explain what research cues have led you to conclude that your case does or does not have negative history.

Has this case generated any positive history? As you will recall, "positive history" means the case has been upheld on appeal and/or otherwise been favorably applied or discussed in a subsequent, unrelated case. Briefly (in one or two sentences) explain what cues have led you to conclude that your case does or does not have any positive history.

Do NOT sign off yet. Stay on the Keycite page to complete Part C below.

C. CONDUCTING A NATURAL LANGUAGE SEARCH USING WESTLAW

Step 1: Formulate your search

Turn back to your LexisNexis exercise on page 48. Beginning with your Boolean search terms from your LexisNexis exercise, create a new phrase in plain language that will reflect the partner's question. Write this new phrase or sentence in the space below.

Step 2: Select your Database and the Natural Language Function

From the Keycite page you were using when you completed Part B of this Assignment, click on the tab on the top center of the screen that says "Directory." Alternatively, you may click Law School or Westlaw on the upper left side of the screen and then click on the "View Westlaw Directory" link at the left side of the screen. Use the links in the directory to narrow your database to the one that most closely matches the database you used in the LexisNexis exercise. Your path likely will be to "U.S. State Materials," then to your particular state, then to "Cases."

 TIP: As you become more experienced with Westlaw, you may learn the abbreviations for the databases and you may not need to use the directory.

 TIP: In certain states where large bodies of water are less common, or where otherwise directed by your instructor, you may choose to search for law in a neighboring state or in a database that combines state and federal cases.

Once you are on the search screen, click "Natural Language" at the top of the Search Terms box.

Step 3: Enter your search phrase in the Search Terms Box

Type your phrase into the Search Terms box and press enter.

Did your natural language search find cases? _____

Which method (Natural Language or Boolean) seems to produce the best results for this particular research question? Why do you think so?

Step 4: View and Print your Research Trail

Westlaw's "Research Trail" function saves your searches and allows you to go back to the results later. Original results can be viewed again at no extra charge until 2 a.m. the next day, and search histories are saved for fourteen days.

Click on "Research Trail" at the top right of any Westlaw screen. When your research trail appears, click on "Download Trail" at the top right of the list. Click "Download" and then select "Print" from the File menu. Attach a copy of your Research Trail to this page of this Assignment.

Step 5: **Sign Off**

Remember to click on the "Sign Off" button when you have completed this part of the your Assignment.

D. DISCOVERING OTHER ELECTRONIC RESOURCES

Background Information: The presence of the Internet has changed the way all of us access information, and its impact on legal research is just as great. As with all internet research, accessing legal information online requires the use of caution and common sense in discerning the accuracy and reliability of the information you gather online. Consider your source and how frequently information is updated before depending on it either as a useful tool to gather background information before launching a search on a fee-based service, or as a source of primary law itself.

Following is an illustrative listing of some of the many reliable internet sites maintained by various entities that can be used to conduct legal research.

> **TIP:** In addition to these sites, a diligent researcher can uncover many other sources including blogs associated with legal scholars, politicians, and journalists, as well as local community websites containing information online ranging from tax and real property records to the full texts of local ordinances and regulations.

Subscription Sites (Sites requiring users to pay a fee for service)

- LexisNexis (www.lexis.com)

- Westlaw (www.westlaw.com)

- Loislaw (www.loisl)

- VersusLaw (www.versuslaw.com)

- Hein-OnLine (http://heinonline.org)

- Casemaker (offered on many state bar association websites for association members)

> **TIP:** Many of the subscription sites have agreements with law schools that provide law students free access. Ask your law librarian or instructor for more information.

Compilation Sites (Sites providing links to other internet sources of legal information)

- The Legal Information Institute at Cornell Law School (www.law.cornell.edu)

- Washburn University School of Law (www.washlaw.edu)

- Findlaw (www.findlaw.com)

Court and Government Sites[4] (Sites provided by various government offices and courts. In addition to these sites of general interest, many state and federal administrative agencies and local governments maintain web pages with legal information.)

- State websites (maintained independently by each state) (www.state.____.us) (insert state's postal abbreviation in place of blank)

- Supreme Court of the United States (www.supremecourtus.gov)

- Federal Courts (www.uscourts.gov)

- Individual Circuit Courts (www.ca____.uscourts.gov) (insert Circuit number 1-11 in place of blank)

- DC Circuit Court: (www.cadc.uscourts.gov)

- Federal Circuit: (www.fedcir.gov)

- Federal Legislative Information – THOMAS – including bills and full text of Congressional documents (http://thomas.loc.gov)

- Government Printing Office – U.S. Code, Code of Federal Regulations, Federal Register, Congressional Record, mid-1990's to present (www.gpoaccess.gov)

Step 1: Select and visit a website that is appealing to you from the list set out above.

---

[4]In addition to these truly free government websites, PACER (Public Access to Court Electronic Records) is available to the public at http://pacer.psc.uscourts.gov. From PACER, researchers can obtain case and docket information from most Federal Appellate, District, and Bankruptcy courts, and from the U.S. Party/Case Index. There is a per-page charge to view documents, and a password is required.

Step 2: In the space below, or on a separate piece of paper attached to this page of this Assignment, describe the primary features of the site you have discovered:

Step 3: In what way might you (or someone to whom you would recommend the site) use this site in the future?

E. USING ONLINE TUTORIALS

Background Information: Becoming confident and competent in your use of LexisNexis and Westlaw takes time (and energy), and is an ongoing, lifetime challenge. To help keep subscribers abreast of the multitude of constantly changing resources and functions available through their services, both Westlaw and LexisNexis provide sophisticated online tutorials.

Step 1: Choose *either* Westlaw *or* LexisNexis, and sign on.

Step 2: Locate a link on the service you have selected to its online tutorials. Note that you may (or may not) need to go to the "for law students" website for either Westlaw or LexisNexis to locate useful tutorials. Tutorials generally can be found using the "Help" menu or the "Site map" link.

Step 3: Select a tutorial on a topic that is of interest to you and complete that tutorial now. In the space below, or on a separate sheet of paper attached to this page of this Assignment, describe the tutorial and how it might be valuable to another student.

Congratulations! You have learned to perform basic online research using Westlaw and LexisNexis, you have become familiar with the wide variety of online resources available to a legal researcher, and you have learned how to access tutorials online for either Westlaw or LexisNexis. If you want additional practice using Westlaw or LexisNexis, turn to page 29 of this Supplement for another chance to try your skills.

Please note your actual time of completion (including background reading): _____ *hrs.*